Thirteen Moons and a Day

Poems on Seasons Relived

Thirteen Moons and a Day

Poems on Seasons Relived

by

Bob Ambrose, Jr.

Cover design by Shay Culligan
Cover image by Tony Detroit
Author photo by Sarah Ambrose

ISBN: 979-8-90146-716-9
Library of Congress Control Number: 2026931922

Kelsay Books
502 South 1040 East, A-119
American Fork, Utah 84003
Kelsaybooks.com

Dedicated to the Nature Ramblers
at the State Botanical Garden of Georgia

Seeking what we find

Acknowledgments

Three poems were first published in *Journey to Embarkation—A Refection in Poetry* (Parsons Porch Books, 2016): "A Sunday Afternoon Island Dream," "The Grace of Late Autumn," "Last November Sunset." They have been revised for this collection.

Two poems were published (in English and Spanish) by *La Gaceta Parnasus:* "Even Sister Mosquito," "A Psalm of Gaia."

"Foreword: The Memory of an Unspoiled Georgia" was excerpted from *Travels Through North and South Carolina, Georgia, East and West Florida* by William Bartram, published in Philadelphia by James and Johnson, 1791, and available through Project Gutenberg.

Many poems in this book were inspired and informed by the Nature Ramblers at the State Botanical Garden of Georgia, led by naturalists Linda Chafin, Dale Hoyt, Don Hunter, Hugh Nourse, Carol Nourse, Anne Shenk, and members of the group. I am deeply grateful for their weekly companionship, their care for nature, and for all they have taught me.

Contents

EPILOGUE

PROLOGUE

May you savor the spirit of each new hour
as minute by minute the moments flow

Foreword: The Memory of an Unspoiled Georgia

How harmonious and sweetly murmur the purling rills and fleeting brooks, roving along the shadowy vales passing through dark, subterranean caverns, or dashing over steep rocky precipices, their cold, humid banks condensing the volatile vapors, which falling coalesce in crystalline drops, on the leaves and elastic twigs of the aromatic shrubs and incarnate flowers!

In these cool, sequestered, rocky vales, we behold the following celebrated beauties of the hills: fragrant [sweet shrub], blushing [Rhododendron], delicate [mock orange], which displays the white wavy mantle, with the sky robed Delphinium, perfumed [lily-of-the-valley] and fiery Azalea, flaming on the ascending hills or wavy surface of the gliding brooks. . . . Clusters of the blossoms cover the shrubs in such an incredible profusion on the hill sides, that suddenly opening to view from dark shades, we are alarmed with the apprehension of the hills being set on fire.

—William Bartram, 1791

Preface: For One More Dance

Precisely timed by atomic clocks
and charted through the course of time,
twelve new moons still wax and wane
each circuit of Earth around its star.

Their dance is etched in the heavens,
  a *pas de trois* long foreordained.

Ah, but the seasons!
Eight
once graced my Southern home.
They sauntered
through each living year
dismissive
of crisp divisions, nodding
casually
at the calendar.

Oh how I've ached for the way it was
  with bodies constructed of spit and dust
    bearing the sea in our blood.

The swing of the moon was in our bones,
  the spin of the Earth, the orbit of Sol.

Our thoughts were froth on a salty gale.

Our tiny lives were shooting stars,
  flaring arcs across the void.

Though most found home in the holy beyond
spurning their berth in the cycles of Earth,
I chose what is holy in both.

So if I could inhabit my body again
blessed for thirteen moons and a day,
I would blaze a trail to the Georgia hills
and dance in the garden of Gaia.

Prelude: To Taste of Life

Give me winter, for instance,
   when the chilling wind finally stills
      and frosty nights grip the hills of Georgia.

Set me on a rustic path
   that winds beyond abandoned barns
      through broomsedge fields of tan and amber

walking with my once-young family
   trailing happy farmhouse dogs
      to picnic on the distant ridge

of weathered granite strewn with boulders,
   lichens, moss, and soft grass beds
      cleansed in the scent of a cedar glade.

Then ease me into early spring
   when bloodroot bloom by woodland streams
      and toads sing love from lowland swamps.

Or the day before the canopy closes
   when nature paints an Impressionist scene
      in tender greens and textures of red.

Put me on a front porch swing
   as ceiling fans slowly stir
      another lush midsummer evening

soaking my bones in moist heat
   watching children chase fireflies
      as twilight sinks into night.

Grant again a golden fall
   of richness tinged with a pensive mood
      when crickets turn a plaintive tune,

a choir of blackbirds sings adieux,
   and hickories fling their dried-up leaves.
      Grant faith to fly with the freshening breeze.

And when my seasons end at last
   as seasons will, I only ask a year's reprieve
      to taste of life again, again.

WHEN LIFE BREATHES LIGHT

To be present in creation
weightless as the moment itself

The Short Side

When Cold Moon lights the longest night
we're on the short side
of the sun.

These are the days of dusk
when the pale sun
beats west

through half-hearted arcs
to warm a far-off
southern sea

and Orion rises, red-shouldered
east into evening
to hunt the midnight sky.

This is the season of silhouettes,
when dark forms
cast shadows

on a velvet void
to illumine by absence
a vast empty realm

where love lies below layers,
faith stands by frozen,
and hope taunts the dormant heart.

This is the grace of unknowing,
the stage beyond belief and doubt,
a place to bank the fire and wait.

Till Ice Moon lights late winter nights
we're on the short side
of the sun.

Becoming the Color of Winter

When the world tilts toward darkness
   and seasons of color wane,
      as you feel life ebbing, look for me:

I am the glint on evergreens
   lit against the clear embrace
      of cold air cleansed on Arctic ice.

I am the swath of bare terrain
   of ochre earth and umber mud
      softened in a misting rain.

I'm the stubble field of muted tan
   suffused in amber overtones
      streaked with shades of fading sun.

I'm the warmth of dancing light
   above a base of burning embers
      cradled in layers of ash.

I am the dome of blue-black sky
   and the glow of a full Wolf Moon
      spilling silver on the sea.

Deep into a sleepless night
   on the bitter edge of winter,
      I will be your summer dream

of sea-green tinged with deep blue hues
   framed by sunbeams slicing through storms
      that rumble along the horizon.

In the Wake of Winter Storms

Savor the stillness
when snow flurries cease
and cling to the peace

of gray-softened sky
when the world casts no shadows.
It never persists.

The polar vortex dips
and the high arctic bursts
through the Plains.

It bears down hard.
It barrels east, closing in
from over the unseen horizon.

Soon the clearing wind,
then the frigid sun.
Tonight the crippling freeze.

Life is a sigh
engulfed by the ages,
an ember that fades into night.

Though hints of transcendence
surround us unseen, though visions
come veiled with the dawn,

these worlds of serenity slip
through the moments and melt
in the wake of winter storms.

Winter Clarity

Bright cold blows thin,
piercing the surface, sweeping the chaff,
clearing out the unfit things.

Winter is a harsh gardener—it culls
the unworthy, the weak, the worn,
so only the strong survive to spring.

I layer up and step outside.
Though bitter wind stings my ears and cracks my skin,
deep within, my spirit quickens.

Summer leaves crunch underfoot
as I move through a still-life of senescence.
Dormant vines hug the high limbs of sleeping trees.

Skirting heaps of brittle twigs
around a shattered, rotting trunk,
I snake my way downslope

to snarls of greenbriar and privet
choking the lowland in frozen profusion.
I clear a swath till my will succumbs.

As cold sun cuts a flawless sky
I shrink beneath the frigid glare
that pierces my pretensions. Friend,

call me old and weak, unworthy,
soul of dust and wind-borne chaff,
but I am an agent of nature as well

rooting out privet to free a green fern
huddled in bottomland duff.
Oh, spring is still a distant shore

but hid beneath these brittle forms
and tucked inside this dry tangle
abundance bides midwinter’s embrace.

Waiting for Dawn and the Sunday Times

My kitchen is so cold I crack
   the oven inches open, crank
the knob to rod-glows-red,
   and hug my hot water bottle.

Pre-dawn drips darkness
   as I watch the eternal sunrise
sweep across the Atlantic
   on my world daylight app.

Silhouettes emerge outside
   as the great arc of light
with an apex above Iceland
   kisses the shores of Georgia.

It is midday in Spain
   and sunset in Sri Lanka,
afternoon in Abu Dhabi,
   midnight in Sydney.

China lies in darkness
   while Auckland inhabits
tomorrow. We share
   the same moment, I muse

while watching out for all
   the news that's fit to print
to hit my driveway double
   wrapped against the drizzle.

I scroll the social media
   past the cats and dinner pics,
by the snark and sentiment,
   around the pronouncements

and dodgy links, to plunge
   through a blog on Buddhism
tagged with a holy aspiration:
   Have light, will travel.

How nice, if only, I mutter,
   startled by the gray brown
world bathed in soft dawn
   as if from within. I check

my app and sure enough,
   it's right on time. Light
comes as new days must,
   to all who sit and wait.

A January Retreat

There are sullen winter spells
that settle heavy on the soul
like overcooked comfort food

on two hour naps
through half dark days
stuck in a string of gray thirties

when silent songbirds cling to trees
and muffled crows cast about, listless.
But, yes—when the cold cloud lifts

I shall head south on a state road
past brown fields of dog fennel
when backlit tips wear tan halos

behind stubble ditches and broomsedge shoulders.
I'll sail over silhouettes of distant cattle
plying well-trod pasture, past tin-roof sheds

strewn about with farm machines,
above old lawns anchored by scotch broom
and lonely oak, over ordered rows of old pecan

outside the town where Remus broods.
I'll crest the fall line and roll
the frozen swells of an ancient seabed

that stretches beyond the blue-green horizon
of barren plantations in cash-crop pine.
Will you come too?

Shall we tune our souls to a mellow song?
Can we *Let it Be Sweet Baby James*
down *The Long and Winding Road* again?

So calm we are energized by Enya.
So centered we bless the car that cuts us off
and send our love to the driver inside.

For there are kind winter spells,
and we are heading south,
cutting through noon shadows

to a land of graybeard and ghosts,
confluence of earth and sky,
river and sea, where brackish channels

braid marsh and mudbank,
porpoise feed the peaceful waters,
and mist mingles with heaven at dawn.

On the Idea of Otters

Once again I do not see otters
   as I walk my old dog west
on the loop trail through winter
   woods to shoals and sunset.

I scan the width of gray chop,
   the white froth hugging rocks,
the slipstreams of submerged logs,
   but all I see is surface churn.

The sun sets somewhere
   behind layers of gray as I listen
for the tell-tale chirp. All is quiet
   save the steady shush, so I turn

back east and follow the brown
   bounce of a hungry dog heading
toward dinner. Today I missed
   the otters again, though I searched

with due sincerity. But once
   on an otherwise scripted morning
in the midst of an unremarkable year
   I watched a romp of river puppies

swim upstream into fall.
   The sun froze mid-sky as I stood
on the bank for minutes or hours
   transfixed by whiskers and wakes.

Wonders once revealed remain
   hidden. We may glimpse visions.
We may tiptoe into thin terrain,
   but all we keep is absence and

what spirit haunts an afterglow.
   Today I walked an old dog down
a winter trail to an empty river
   and muffled sunset, and found

they suffice, for I carry the image
   of otters. Ever since their presence
etched an ordinary day, it's now
   enough to know they are there.

Reading on My Deck One Balmy Winter Day

I was interrupted by a sunset
of the understated kind—
ragged layers of gray overlain
by islands of off-white sky.

I don't remember when,
but the wind had died.
Not a breath disturbed the bare tips
and twisted limbs of winter trees

while underneath, the whole
world shone. Nothing you
could capture by camera,
nothing to inspire a song.

A gentle river washed the world
with white noise, a still spell
soon cracked by the call
of a Carolina wren. Listen,

we live only moments
and notice so few. Will you
close the book? Would you
shut down the screen? Look,

night sweeps from the east
beyond the speed of sound.
Gray deepens a shade. Dull
lace of red maple darkens.

The cream sky turns coral.
Shadows merge. Somehow
creation holds together. Even
in darkness the world glows.

The Catkin Edge

As catkins swell the tips of alder,
red-fringed auras of riverside maple
soften the edge of winter.

A new breeze lifts the grip
of late-stage February. Deep beneath
the dead brown leaves, spirits gather.

I wish these days would hurry on—
my mother's presence pierces years to conjure sun
and wrap the world in warmer tones.

And I hear his gentle rejoinder,
that faux-scold timbre tinged with a twinkle—
Don't wish your only life away.

Dad was the ever-enduring hills. She,
an effervescent air-kiss, the smiles and dreams
of springs to come. Now both are gone.

I throw on a warm layer,
zip inside my black hoodie, and huddle
out back in a broken pool of light,

wishing with mother for everwarmth
and winter's end, but feeling my father's calm
as if from distance. Stay

and wash my soul in cold breeze
beneath this bare-branch blackbird tree
on the catkin edge of wintertime.

Reverie on the End of Winter

Grace is a bush full of bees
in a February garden
bathed in the fragrance of a honeysuckle spring.

It's the mellow chords of acoustic guitar
wafting down a grassy slope
wrapped in a melody of love.

Grace is a joy of children
skipping up a sunlit hill,
chatter-laughing an unknown tongue.

It shakes the world with playful yelps
that wake the winter buds,
enticing ancient bones to dance.

Grace is the song of the mourning dove,
the soft call from distance
that soothes the memory of decades gone.

It's the amber leaves of American beech
shining through an understory
brushed with afternoon light.

Or the lavender hue of hepatica
that pokes through oak litter
on the bank of an unnamed creek.

I did not earn this day.

But the woods still beckon
with textures of brown
and sinuous contours bare to the sky.

And still the river glides south,
swirling by sand bars, gurgling past snags,
casting eddies toward a distant sea.

Spring Before Leaf-Out

Signs belie the still-bare branches
arching the hardwood forest with an airy weave.
Can you hear the hickory clear his throat?
Inside the shaggy bark, cells repair

and pipes revive. Buds swell the tips of twigs.
High on a rough trunk, resurrection ferns go green.
Maples blush tawny red.
Spring seeps inside the trees.

My calendar shows a winter scene
with numbers tucked in ordered rows
but birds know better.
Did you catch the morning chatter?

Out of darkness, cardinals sing
and wrens respond with small bird bluster.
Can you hear the new tenor?
Spring is in the daybreak song.

The dirt below us lives—
can you feel the tremor?
A scattering of small flowers push white
through the brown litter blanket.

Here, the bloodroot. Here, hepatica.
There, the hairy bittercress.
Golden ragwort bud purple by a fungus-crusted log.
Spring comes first to humble lives.

It creeps in cold.
It calls you from your long torpor.
Will you kneel down by tiny flowers?
Will you tread lightly the altar of Earth?

On the First Wave of Spring

You may sense a strange lightness
inside your bones. Unseen, life
is rising. Unheard, Earth hums.

And so it comes,
the imperceptible turn
when winter tips to early spring.

First it stirs.
It seeps through roots.
It creeps on marbled salamander feet.

It emerges from burrows,
arises from mud,
ascends into shifting winds.

It slithers onto shallow rocks,
peers from gaps in mossy logs,
rustles under leaf litter.

It chitters from trees,
trills from swamps,
and peeps from vernal pools.

It shivers, and saucer magnolias bloom,
pears and cherries wear blossoms of snow,
and redbuds slip into hot pink lace.

It smiles, and forsythia shine,
each bush a burst of golden stars
in a firmament of baby green leaves.

It laughs, and daffodils dance again.
They sway to the slipstreams of speeding cars
and swirl in the clefts of exit ramps.

And in the rhythms of wind and light
across the parks and small-town squares—
the breath of Earth, the dance of life.

Myrtle Warblers

You may call them butter butts
(they are not diminished). Perhaps
you'll catch an idle glimpse

looking out from the kitchen sink
as the spring waves muster.
The flocks move out by night

flying north in the cold light
of a late March moon. They go
about their business by day

skimming insects from rivers,
gleaning from leaves,
stealing from spiderwebs.

The strong will make their way
under a mellow April moon.
By May they'll arrive, warbling

the northern woods in summer.
They'll flit through conifer stands
flashing butter yellow rump,

then flood the continent in fall
from the great blue-green spruce
down ancestral flyways.

In the dearth of winter they'll settle
into Southern scrub, Eastern woods,
and mountain hollows

to digest the wax from myrtle berries.
Someone must—it's a niche,
and who's to say a minor role?

For there is a final dignity to it all,
a calling in the cogs and cycles,
the bones and blood of Gaia.

The Business of High Spring

The soulful notes of a wood thrush cease
when coded warnings cut the air.

A hawk swoops through the understory
culling anoles and unwary mice.

Chipmunks skitter for hidden dens.
A buzzard wheels overhead.

Shadows and silence . . .
The bustle resumes.

Beauty is a privileged vision
in a world hard about business—

where nervous squirrels vie for the rights
to your bird feeder

and goldfinches fight for the tattered sack
of thistle seed.

Where biting flies rise from brush
and chiggers infest the meadows.

They covet your blood
for you, too, are a creature of spring.

You are the doe and deer tick,
the moth and the evening swallow.

You are the red-shouldered hawk
and the unfortunate field mouse too slow to his hole.

You are the quickest chipmunk,
the first finch on a thistle bag,

the orphaned fawn, the crippled wren,
bones and feathers pecking the dirt.

You're the squirrel chased back to her perch
chattering oaths and scratching fleas.

You are the starboard hind flank flea
and the chigger that missed her mark.

Spring is open air improv ballet.
Its beauty is hard business.

A Springtime Apparition

Clayton, North Carolina

By the barely greening side yard pecan,
crepe myrtle and magnolia grace
the Southern small-town spring.

Paradise is a pool of cool air
infused with essence of mown grass
and the scent of sweet Carolina jessamine.

A mockingbird-freight train duet
weaves a Sunday morning sermon
as an old dog ambles to the edge

of his chain-link fence. Sensing stranger,
he barks without conviction.
From the unseen center, church

bells carry hymns of hope
to whoever wanders
a fresh apparition of Eden.

Through the Windows of Spring

When nights drift through open windows
   and you wake to mornings enveloped in green,
      the world is a nursery with you again

the grass-stained boy hopping rocks
   by a slow creek that winds through
      the idylls of childhood. Or the lithe girl

in scruffy jeans clutching a rough trunk
   halfway up the side yard plum
      which thrives on the edge of an unruly lawn.

Aroma of onion grass spikes the air
   as you weave a bouquet of dandelions
      and skip to a medley of mockingbird tunes.

You wander once more through living woods
   where tangles of jessamine hang from the trees
      and armies of iris encircle the ponds.

You gaze in wonder at street-side weeds
   where scattered arcs of Dove's-foot flowers
      make lavender galaxies tangled in green.

And you rest again on a carpet of clover
   woven with tendrils of purple vetch
      in the spell of a flowering dogwood.

You are the boy now covered in mud,
   the girl with a jessamine necklace.
      You slip through the windows of spring.

Lament for a Rose-Breasted Grosbeak

He died in the height of a Georgia spring
   on a garden morning green as Eden
when the slant of sunlight warms the wings
   and lifts a feast of flying insects.

Far from his tropical winter retreat,
   he'd crossed the Gulf on a perilous night
and followed unfolding canopies north,
   drawn toward summer breeding grounds.

But never made it. In a spell of delight
   he dipped below a break in the woods,
swooping and swerving for food, for joy.
   Wide blue skies were in his sight.

The end was abrupt. He banked
   hard into high glass—dead
before he hit the ground.
   Rose-breasted beauty fell at my feet.

I cradled his warmth in my aging hands
    to will his broken body back. My hope
was vain—billions fall in the flyways
    in a world diminished bird by bird.

Mid-Spring Comes to Small Town South

With the waxing of the Flower Moon
and softening of the dawn,
languid days settle in.

Last frost is long past. Fierce storms
soak freshly-plowed fields and puddle
country roads. Kitchen gardens sprout.

In the back of weathered mansions
and beside abandoned shacks alike,
Chinaberry bursts into pale purple hues.

Honeysuckle scents a gentle breeze
and wisteria drapes weary trees
with a heavy lavender shroud.

Weeks break in fragrant waves.
Fields that featured buttercup
streak yellow ragwort now.

These are the days of white clover
when raucous bands of dandelion
stalk the slopes of suburban lawns.

This is the time the tanager returns
flitting red through high branches
amidst a hundred shades of green.

This is the season of tender leaves
when cool winds sift the canopy
with a soothing woodland sigh.

The world teems with calls and songs,
lilts and *chortles, wheets* and *teeters,*
chucks, clucks, caws and *cheers.*

Now is the time of new life. Why
should I keep from singing?

A Dream on Reading Bartram

Sometimes I shut my eyes and see
a Southern piedmont stream run clear

from misty heights of the Cherokee
through woodlands of Muskogee Creek.

In dreams I hear the hymn of rills
that whisper from the ancient glades.

I wander with Bartram through shadowy vales
and breathe again their sweet perfumes.

The hills are robed in Delphinium blues
and white wavy mantles of mock orange shrubs.

There on the banks of a hidden brook
where vapors condense into crystalline drips

we savor the fragrance of sweetshrub flowers
framed by the flaming azaleas of May.

But when I wake, his world has gone
from forest paths to asphalt streets

where English ivy creeps from lawns
to strangle tame suburban trees.

Now Chinese privet crowds the sills
of silted rivers, clay-stained creeks,

and kudzu casts a tangled shroud
across the red, eroded hills.

This broken land I love cries out
from shadows of what could have been.

Gossamer Fossils

We often walked a woodland trail
that wound beside these river shoals.
Now I linger alone on the shadowy bank
where long ago on a sultry day

I sat in the shade lulled by a breeze
while my dogs dug into humus
and bedded down in cool dirt
to savor the bottomland scent.

Once again I ease into a reverie
watching water rushing by
the rock-strewn reach
to sculpted pools
where dappled sunlight
filters through the hidden depths
that harbor life
beneath the stream-side canopy.

I hear the ethereal
waterthrush
calling from a hidden perch
and the same bold notes
of wren-song
beyond the old gneiss boulder
patched with moss
and lichens.

I sense a presence lost in time
that haunts the ever-fresh present.
It seems to bear the sadness
of moments buried years ago.

I feel a fleeting sweetness, too,
condensed from bits of memory,
those gossamer fossils left by a living web
that binds our souls with unseen thread.

A Springtime Promise

There are springtime Saturdays bursting with birdsong and breeze so sweet no set of sun salutations, no hymn of praise could say such love. When life breathes light, and you run for hours on joy alone. Do not forget these days.

For there will be fortnights
      filled
         with fail
   when the world assaults

your spirit with chainsaws
      at eight
         sharp
   on days that follow

frantic weeks of sleep
      denied
         when fears
   converge on fitful nights

when cynicism drains
      your life
         your heart
   grows dim beneath bright

skies which mock your
      lonely
         soul
   with lies that love

persists and life abides
      for flesh
         is grass
   that withers, dries

when summer brings
      its scorching
         breath
   and blows untethered

hope to shreds. Do not
      forget
         the spring.
   For there will be seasons

when you find yourself
dark pilgrim
plunging
through too many

tomorrows, so lost
salvation
is just
a set of syllables

in some forgotten tongue
when paths
wind inward,
spiral aimless, down

through tangles, torn
      convictions,
         worn out
   dreams, forsaken, trapped

in mental mazes, soul
      cries out
         against the ages,
   curses life, denies it twice,

that broken vessel
      born to die.
         Do not
   forget the darkest times.

But there will be springtime Saturdays when you find your heart strangely calm, when the sacred surrounds you with signs, for it's written on the lattice of a late season frost and whispered in the midnight storm that peace, perhaps, will find you yet, perhaps for you a pulse and breath, for you the tilt and turn of Earth, for you a patch of morning sun.

Spring's End

As surely as Earth tilts toward the sun
the long spring slumps into summer.

Today the pastel sunrise
tints the cirrus wisps in pink.

Soon the sky will glow again
with the radiance of late May.

Now the catalpa is covered in white.
Now the southern magnolia blooms.

Gardenia sweetness drifts on a breeze
bearing a fragrant bouquet.

The scented air soothes my skin,
softens my heart, loosens my soul.

My gaze expands beyond my sight
to high in the hardwoods, hidden by leaves

where chickadees feast on an insect buffet
and nestlings beg for a share.

The limbs are alive with spiders and mites
in a canopy crawling with aphids

trailing their sweet organic sheen.
A hickory is dripping the sticky dew

onto the frame of my Ford, a sign
that spring has run its course.

Time to retreat to the edges of night—
A hundred days of heat ahead.

A Prayer of June in Green and Brown

To be present in creation
   weightless as the moment itself

when eternity is an in-breath
   of early June evening
as life hums a low note
   and soft shafts of fading light
caress the deepening shade.

Or the pool of morning
   when bug-trill and birdsong
weave the treetops,
   waking whole days.

Or in the still-breath,
   when slant yellow
renders shades of green
   to veins of gold
and the nervous wren
   pauses on a porch rail
regarding options.

   He fans a tiny wing,
   darts eyes, twitches
   twice, flies. Action

breaks the idle spell, restores
   the world to green and brown.

I do not trust a golden throne
  guarded by pearl-encrusted gates—

just give me *Now* in my out-breath
  and God in the garden, weaving
    dew beads for a new solstice.

On the Care and Feeding of Rodents

There's a squirrel on my bird feeder
   scarfing a batch of sunflower seeds
meant for a tufted titmouse
   and a faithful pair of chickadees.

But hidden on the kitchen deck—
   a fully loaded water cannon
dripping from the business end.
   The boy inside me smiles.

I shoulder the Stream Machine
   Hydrobolic Water Launcher
and take my righteous aim—
   justice shall be served wet.

The thief is hanging upside down,
   hind feet clutching top bar struts,
front paws clawing side-wire mesh.
   I see she's a mama, and freeze,

recalling a cold winter evening
   in the old Oglethorpe farmhouse
when my wife caught the kitchen
   mouse in a live trap. It was late,

so she placed the pest in a Mason jar.
   Morning saw the slick rodent nursing
a litter of newborn pups. The fate
   of generations hung in kindly hands.

Guess who fashioned a luxury nest
   in a snug corner of an unused barn
stocked with water and nuts. Hint:
   the bond between mamas is strong.

Swept by a fit of chivalry, I lower the soaker
   and toss a handful of peanuts instead.
Mama scoots down the slippery pole
   (greased last week to no avail).

As she scampers away with a roasted prize
   my inner boy sighs and scans for snakes.
A chickadee alights on the repurposed feeder.
   If ever the peaceable kingdom would come

it could start in a corner of creation where
   songbirds and squirrels share in the bounty
next to a kitchen deck. Do you hear the call?
   I'm off to Kroger for peanuts and seeds.

The Eternal News of Early June

In memory of Dale Hoyt

Come, my friend, just one last time
and walk me down a Garden path
reliving a ramble in early June

when once again a hummingbird house
is wound in silk and saliva. Describe
how it's layered with lichens and leaves

then show where it hides
high in a white oak
cloaked in a canvas of green.

Come weave a tale of hungry toads
hunting the musty leaf-littered dampness
under the air-dance of damselflies.

Then mimic the trill of a Leopard frog
and the plucked *glunk* of its Green cousin
calling from a froggy shore.

Now talk me through the gruesome fate
of zombie bugs riddled with fungus
clinging to leaf-tip graves.

Speak of the hidden lives in soil—
of thousand-gendered mycelia
and subterranean slime-mold sex.

Then show me the home of chanterelles
where gold funnels grow
on a green moss floor.

Bring on the air of an early summer
bounding through a boyhood day
recalling the ways of wonder

and watch me shed my decades
like the sloughed skin of an aging snake
baking in the noonday sun.

Come the twist of eternity
let us idle outside the gates of heaven
to drift in the peace of a warm summer breeze.

On Early Summer Elderwalks

I hike through my neighborhood
   in the guise of an old man
with just a hint of a gimpy hip.
   Gripping a gnarled walking stick,

I'm out before the heat
   huffing up hills,
passed by young runners
   and mothers rolling strollers.

They nod in my general direction
   smiling past the half-seen elder.
We share the same street
   but live in different worlds.

I walk as much in memory
   as in the searing moment.
I slip through years,
   misplace whole decades.

I zig-zag through shadows
   and pause in a pool of shade.
A warm breeze sifts the mimosa
   and I breathe its pink sweetness.

I scan the borders of ragged lawns
   telling sumac from senna,
cat's-ear from dandelion,
   wild petunia from woodland phlox.

I rest my eyes on morning glory
   trailing intricate lavender blooms
from vines that twist and twine toward light
   and tendrils that spill over fences.

Drawn to calls of *Hey Mr. Bob*
   from a lawn full of children at play,
I watch their beloved Wally
   snatch a flying frisbee in stride.

As morning warms, a low drone fills
   the distance. With sun high on my back,
I saunter home through the green
   aroma of fresh-mown grass.

On the other side of sunset I walk
   my wife past a field of fireflies
tracing seductive J-shaped loops
   as signs of love in the failing light.

We stroll in the silence of so many years
   that merge as we turn toward home.
A half century of Strawberry Moons
   soften my twilight sky.

Swept in the spell of affection, I nudge
   a young snake with the tip of my stick.
The copperhead coils, then flows
   off the asphalt into the night.

The Scent of a Summer Storm

Falling drops are free of fragrance.
The ethereal scent of a gentle rain

is only the oil exuded by plants
and aromatics escaping the earth.

That bracing whiff of wind-whipped sea—
just dimethyl sulfides and aerosols of salt.

Ah, but I've basked in the tang
that hangs over oceans. I have bathed

in the fragrance of fresh fallen rain
as splattered essence of earth arose

with the force of a living moment.
I've breathed in the sweetness

released from the dirt and learned
of a truth I cannot constrain,

an elation untamed by explanation,
a joy that cannot be named.

When you dance in the rain would it tarnish
the spell to know it's only petrichor?

Heron World

Late afternoon hangs a still life
of shade, sunlight, and sky
draped with veils of moist heat
that leave a sheen on glistened skin.

And as the river valley glows,
the shimmering green
surrounds a solitary
heron

perched in gray-white dignity,
his sleekness suspended
from supple neck
to thin stick legs

inhabiting a heaven
of sparkling mud
and slow waters
that flow through a bend of eternity.

Here at day's end
his gaze remains true
to ripples and darting shadows,
to splash and sustenance below.

Now the heron unfolds
into neck and wing
flashing blue-silver rhythm
in ponderous flight.

Now a harsh cry highlights
    primordial grace
        disappearing in downstream shadow
      as eternity dissolves

       and a light breeze hints
           soft darkness to come.

The Arch of Midsummer

High summer rises from June,
   an Elysian arch of unsure origins
      and indefinite ends. Deep within

the green mirage, yesterday
   reflects tomorrow, tomorrow
      bears the day before.

A living engine hums between.
   To feel the rhythm, to enter in
      the rolling forever, the price

is but a light sweat rambling
   through a ripe morning
      in search of pearls you can

never possess. As in a dream
   with languid gaze, to trace
      the green of a graceful katydid

making like a slender leaf
   sleeping off a late-night gig.
      To pause in a cloud

of sweat bees and butterflies
   lapping the honeydew ooze
      of the aphid. To pass through

the shade of a lowly pawpaw
serviced in spring by carrion
flies, gleaned in the darkness

by agile raccoons and ambling
opossums. Abandon your self
to the sleepy haze, soothed

by the soft hypnotic thrum
of another mid-summer
about the business of Eden again.

INTERLUDE: SUMMER DREAMS OF DISTANT SHORES

Perhaps you'll feel a touch of grace
washed in warm midsummer sun.

A Back Dune Reverie

Ocean Isle, North Carolina

Alone amid the sea oats and beach heather,
just beyond a weathered deck that spans

the back dune scrub, I scan the trampled footpath
that snakes through the sandy gap toward

the sky-blue sea, still glassy in the morning
calm. The curve of the horizon calls

but I stay, toes set in sand like roots of elder
gripping the dunes. Morning sun warms

my neck. I listen to crickets. Gulls careen
overhead as they wind their way to work.

I bless the wren-song, the silent flight of swifts,
the sinuous line of pelicans gliding over

the ocean's edge, tracing ephemeral contours
of air on an ancient unhurried hunt.

Growing up I heard their call while combing
bits of beach debris. A primordial ocean

had woken my soul and I yearned to become
an explorer pursuing blue horizons.

I left footprints on four continents. That life
is a sepia dreamworld etched in salt air.

A sea breeze rises, and I sense a strange calling—
to bloom in hues of rose and gold

and bless the world like firewheel flowers
that grace the nameless back dune plains.

Cloud Play in White on Blue

Bald Head Island, North Carolina

I drift through sleep
on dreams of peace
under the Thunder
Moon of July

then wake up and watch
white cumulus
expanding into
cerulean

I hear the whisper
of palm fronds
rasping secrets
of the sea breeze

then look out and see
white ibis
scouring the shade
of cedar trees

I let go and glide
the summer mind
and sense the impassive
watcher smile

as I trace the fate
of clouds in skies
and grasp the end
of mortal lives—

we all resolve in blue

A Sunday Afternoon Island Dream

Isle La Motte, Vermont

Down at the Fisk farm
four Vermont Yankees
play the blues

to polite applause
beside the art barn
where the well behaved

sip unsweet tea
and lemonade
to wash down

deeply chocolate pie
on lawn chairs pulled
to patchy shade

as laid back bikers glide
slow roads that wind past
fields and cider stands

which operate on honor code
(how goodness goes
in honest lands) where

in the deep late afternoon
a humble man
in holey jeans

strides up the road
with violin and soon
the early evening still

is gently filled
with Air on a G String
as maestro plays

Bach on the beach
with more passion
than skill, much

like most marriages
which get by
on grace and guts

to kinder days
like Isle La Motte
its summertime

ice cider joy
distilled from bitter
winter nights

Boothbay Gray

Boothbay, Maine

If you hold a quiet pose

ankle deep in shallow water
soles set to fine sand

rooted into rising tide
that carved the coves
in the coast of Maine,

perhaps you'll feel a touch of grace
washed in warm midsummer
sun and bathed in the midday
joy-song of brother thrush.

If you hold while tiny crablettes
scuttle-crawl across your feet
and minnows clean your wrinkled toes,
perhaps you'll catch the seaweed sway
to sister moon and lapping wave.

And if you chance to hold your ground
with thighs immersed beneath the tide,
perhaps your pulse will realign,
your breath reset to offshore breeze,
your mind at peace with mother sea.

Perhaps you'll find your soul
submerged within the one eternal
moment, calm as the evening
osprey, who holds a quiet pose

on a pole with a view
to watch the daylight
slowly fade, his world

dissolve in shades of gray
and unobserved, to fly away

as silence fills the fog-bound night.

Haleakala

Maui, Hawaii

From the fertile plain at Pukalani
you ascend the flank of Haleakala
through tall stands of shady koa
to white pine and pasture
scrub bush and boulder
silversword and cinder
sky, wind

realm
of cold light
and piercing shadow
where psyche expands
into the silence of stern truths
rendered in whispers without words

You were given a garden
and precious days,
numbered—
you do not belong here,
but linger
and count the shades
of gold
in the sunset below,
then descend through
darkness
and find your own
fertile plane
to cultivate and sustain
through every ordinary day
that may remain
as servant, helper, partner,
friend.

Pilgrim on Pipiwai Trail

Maui, Hawaii

1.

In sunny clearings
suffused with sweetness,
sour passionfruit, fallen,
offers rich red pulp
shamelessly to all
who would partake
in its cycle.

2.

Nurtured aloft
young banyans survive
by strangling their host
with aerial roots
grasping for ground.

This is their nature—
they can do no else
and participate long
in this world of strife.

But decades are kind
and beginnings fade.
With strength, they mellow,
returning life's blessing.
This is also their nature.

On Pipiwai Trail
a wild banyan
stretches its welcome
to hikers and pilgrims—

Come meditate and laugh
in my playscape of trunks,
on my limbs and roots,
then shelter in the unity
of my singular being.

3.

Under the towering bamboo glade
in a thicket of impenetrable profusion
    lies a portal
brooding in cathedral dimness.

Muted shafts rise
    from a pale litter floor
        to their distant green destiny
            stories above.

            High shoots
              clack and tap
            an otherworldly composition
              as the structure groans
            in ghostly lament
              of a heavy burden
            perpetually borne.

4.

With pounding mechanical power
flying tourists
swoop, circling
to grab their view
Kipahulu Valley
that magnificent painting
silver ribbons
snaking sheer walls
to a canopy carpet
far below.
Satiated, the rumble recedes
and they are gone.

5.

Reality remains behind
where waters spill freely
from a glistening cliff
soaring over a shallow depression
where hikers become pilgrims
of feathery mist.

A humble rock basin
receives the shower
and overflows in abundance
to supply sacred pools far removed.

Stumbling Toward a Brampton Manor

Cumbria, England

When you exit the two-car train
outside the village of Brampton
and leave the lonely platform
tugging wobbly wheeled bags
loaded with too much stuff

the mile or two toward an old manor
which your wife saw on the web
and Google diverts you down a dwindling lane
lined with loosestrife and ragwort
where cattle crowd the mid-day shade

and watch you weary on
till the surface turns to gravel
and your wife and daughter forge ahead
while you tend bags beside the rusting gates
of a deserted dairy farm

composing prayers for traveling mercies
parsing signs and portents
as the Brampton black cat
freezes your soul with yellow-green eyes
and claims your suitcases

well

this is when a lanky farmer named James
ambles up, asks if you're lost
or Canadian
then offers a ride in his sawdust truck
and you choose to trust

because this is Cumbria
and life is good—
your belly's full
and the sun held for one more day.
Tomorrow, let it rain.

Dawn Dreams in a Glasgow Cafe

Glasgow, Scotland

Mid-July and zipped into layers,
I huddle by the high glass walls
of a Sauchiehall Street coffeehouse
on a rain-soaked morning in Glasgow.

It is Sunday. Restless seagulls
patrol the glistened streets. Pigeons
pick manna from cracks in the sidewalk.
Strangers roll suitcases down the damp plaza.

But I dream of the highlands—
forests of birch and pine,
breath of mist and fir.

I kneel in the humus of needles and moss
and ponder the ruins of castles and clans
wrought by the bonnie princes of war.

A puff of wind ruffles the mirror-face
of morning over an inland loch.

I slip out of the chandeliered foyers
and opulent halls of the once important.

Sunlight cascades through cathedral trees
and wavelets kiss the sea-aster shore.

Above villages swollen with summer—
sticky toffee, shops selling tartan—

I climb the bracken hillsides to high heather.
Wind sweeps in from Iceland.
My fingers numb and somehow
it's August.

How soon we haste to the land of before
where dreams devolve to memories,
cropped and cleaned and hung in the hall
by a wide-open door.

Coming Home

My window fogs as we roll
through puddles and primordial mist
down the endless Atlanta tarmac
to the furthest perch in the terminal.

Our packed cabin disgorges the bleary
to the eternal tide of strangers
ebbing down the concourse,
all drawn toward home.

I lug a week's worth of laundry,
small soaps and assorted toiletries
across a vast concrete car-scape
to the last long-term lot.

The way out is wide open.
Soon the city lights fade
in my rearview mirror. Silent
lightning paints the blackened horizon

like a short-circuiting strobe
as I push east, deep into Georgia.
I steer through sleepy towns
to the ragged edge of midnight

where I skirt a deserted campus
and turn down familiar streets.
A dripping redbud arches low
over my darkened driveway.

I cut the engine and pause
as the rhythmic hymn of katydids
and the rasping peep of tree frogs
wash my travel-wracked body.

I hear the hoot of a barred owl
haunting the high limbs of a dying oak
down by the river. My skin tingles
and the bones of my soul sigh, *home.*

WHEN TIME TRENDS TOWARD WANING

There's an ache impressed
on the cosmic tapestry
through the ever-expanding void.
I am is its cry, ever fading.

Jurassic Dreams and Katydids

There is always a week in August
stuck in a musty fold of time,
when the world spins in place

and the season teeters on the brink
as every August that ever was
seeps in the marrow of a single day.

I rise in darkness.
Damp air caresses my skin
as I amble down empty streets listening to crickets.

Furtive songbirds molt in silence.
A doe slips through the shadows of a streetlamp.
The moon dissolves in a bank of haze.

Morning dawns, gray-laden and soft,
tucked with mushrooms, mold and rot,
laced with dew-spun webs.

The sodden hours slip by, dripping,
yet in the dripping, never dry. But mist
burns off by noon, and midday glares.

As sun beats down on bare pavement,
profane hawks shriek obscenities.
A gang of crows loiters in the treetops.

Oblivious gnats hurl their bodies
at unguarded eyes. The world thrums
with the jet-beat of cicada days.

On a primal August such as this
griffinflies stretched their foot-long wings
to hunt Carboniferous swamps.

Red-eyed raptors stalked Jurassic plains,
and monster crocs lay in wait for Cretaceous prey.
They ruled their own unchanging days.

The western sky blackens. Cool
downdrafts shake the canopy. Limbs crack.
A pack of storms sweeps through.

Out my open bedroom window
a sultry evening settles in. Soon,
I think. Soon enough the season turns.

Soon enough it all moves on. I sleep
with the distant night-song of Dilophosaurus
enveloped by ancient tree-tip strumming—

she did—she didn't
        she did—she didn't
                she did—she did—she did

Love Under an August Moon

When the sun has slumped
   through late summer haze
      and dipped beneath the distant hills,

I venture into the evening heat
   to mark another dog day *done.*

As Earth exhales, I watch
   the shadows converge
      till blessed darkness settles in.

A liquid moon
   shimmies
      into the viscous sky

and a twinkling of fireflies
   drifts through the understory
      flashing love at the forest floor.

I hear a tree frog's nasal *quank*
   and soon the rhythmic *scritch* of a cricket.
      A katydid begins to trill.

The night comes alive
   with a passionate cacophony
as hordes of tiny suitors
   pour their souls into courting-song.

A strumming, thrumming,
   rutting bacchanal
pulses through the humid night
   beneath the placid moonglow.

It’s nature’s way—
   how August nights beget
      August nights.

It ends with the hum of exhaustion.

Satiation prevails
   as amber sunlight streaks the east.

I step out early
   to breathe the soft, unsullied dawn.

A chaste world awaits under a pastel sky.

Even Sister Mosquito

Soothed by the *shush*
  of the river shoals,
    from the shade of an oak

in the heat of the day
  a holy peace pervades
    my waking. *Cantiamo*

Saint Francis says,
  then sings with his sisters,
    cicada and thrush.

As he blesses his brothers—
  the worm, the wolf—
    I tingle with feelings

of love for all creatures.
  Would he pray
    for the soul

of sister mosquito
  who tickles my skin
    till I mindlessly slap

and find her exquisite body
  flattened against my flesh?
    A smidge of her saliva

mixed into my blood
   yields a most unholy itch.
      As I scratch my forearm

the reverie snaps,
   and I curse
      her line of forebears

back to Triassic flies.
   They plagued the age
      of dinosaurs with whining

clouds of mouthparts
   wielding needles
      sheathed with saws.

Though your skin may crawl
   at the thought of *Sasquatch*
      stalking forest nights

or *Jaws* patrolling coastal swells,
   save your respect
      for these flimsy pests—

crepuscular hunters,
   hand-maidens to malaria,
      dawn hosts to dengue fever,

for *they* are the hunters
  and *we,* their prey.
    Will we ever be able

to honor their role
  in the cycle of being?
    I slap yet another

then scratch and sigh—only when
  a gentle spirit remakes the Earth
    in the image of Eden—

only then could we honestly utter:
  brother midge, sister mosquito,
    may agape ascend to ahimsa.

Awaiting Passage into Fall

When a Southern August lays on hands,
    a lush embrace of steamy weeks
        sets in before the fall.

Through waning days I run the dawn
    by tidy lawns refreshed with dew.
        Their scent and sparkle stir anew

as memories reconstitute
    old seasons born so long ago
        in stain and sweat and schoolboy pride

forged from summer football trials
    in heat and pads on high school fields
        that to young minds must surely yield

triumphant Friday nights to come
    if only August days would end
        at last in break of fall.

Those rites of passage echo yet
    in aching muscles one-time strong.
        They burn inside my body

decades on as by degrees
    the morning dark seeps into day
        and evening light melts away.

Locked in August once again,
   the weeks pile up as all await
      the break of heat that snaps the spell

while age and darkness creep, encroach,
   and claim their share of fading light
      for passage into fall.

This Mellow Season

Emerging from summer miasma,
I ease my way down a garden path
immersed in a season that has no name.

Earth's tilt has finally taken—shadows
have shifted and nights have cooled.
A fresh yearning stirs the land.

Welcome to the shoulder season
that cleaves the heat of high summer
from the weeks that launch the fall.

It runs through the blossoming of goldenrod
to the rudding of sumac leaves.
It seeds the husks of summer flowers

and ripens muscadine vines,
then rouses a billion birds to flight
and fuels their flyways south.

The season brings a softened light
on gentle days with rose-hued skies
as evenings yield to silver nights

that drift through windows opened wide
to catch the wistful cricket-hymn
that marks their only Harvest Moon.

This mellow season bears no name
    but brings a melancholic balm—
        the tender touch of transience

that blesses those who chance to roam
    with spirits shaped by nature
        and molded much as mine.

When joy deserts a restless soul,
    no intricate doctrine ever devised
        nor absolution could finally provide

        the solace of a rising breeze
    rippling the tips of broomsedge
            in a pasture of bluegrass going to seed.

Weeds Have Names

As a boy exploring the borders
   of Eden I sensed the names
assigned by Adam. But science
   prefers the precision of Latin—

So *Verbesina alternifolia* is an *Asteraceae*
of order *Asterales,* featuring a flower in
the form of *capitula,* surrounded by
involucral bracts.

Weeds have names we'll never know,
   but 'wingstem' sticks to unschooled minds
and 'dog fennel' channels bliss,
   the smell of boyhood forts in fields.

Glory is goldenrod and crownbeard
   when old fields glow yellow
against blue-purple tips of towering ironweed
   and lavender balls of tall thistle.

Peace comes to the cusp of fall
   on white waves of frostweed
and ivory boneset, in pokeweed
   and patches of rabbit tobacco.

By the margins of forest, beautyberry
   thrive and grape ferns unfurl
their sensitive fronds. The world
   bursts with hidden soul

as my back yard goes ragged.
   Elephant foot in exuberance
grows ungainly shoots
   branching through odd angles

to tiny flowers, which lend
   the lawn a purple hue. Weeds
have names we cannot know
   expressed in scent and pollen.

Bumblebees consume their sweetness.
   Fritillaries share their bodies.
They toil and spin their secret lives,
   they reproduce, and soon

they die. We barely sense a hidden
   soul, clothed in rude glory
exceeding kingly robe and throne.
   They make on life a modest claim,

but each one bears its own true name
   known to God and them alone.

Butterfly Time

Before the autumn frost returns
        and fall takes hold of the rolling hills
    sweeping the leavings of summer away

would you linger with me these fleeting weeks?
        Shall we savor the golden days
    swollen with nectar and pollen?

For here in the heat of September
        before a dome of cold descends
    to grip and thin this insect Eden

                no sacred shrine could rival
                a Pipevine Swallowtail,

        no artifact could dazzle
        like a bush of Fiery Skippers,

                    no gilded throne could thrill my soul
                    like a Monarch on a milkweed,

            and nothing made by man could match
            a sunlit field of Sulphurs.

When we pause beside a Joe Pye weed
        in a cloud of Painted Ladies,
    we are pilgrims in a holy place

and should we dare to humble ourselves
to share the land with the least,
we may find ourselves the astonished guests

at the *Festival* of insects,
the *Feast Season* for spiders,
and the *High Holy Days* for butterflies.

Aftermath

When the outer band of Irma arrives, we light a candle
and ride the night storm in a soft cinnamon glow.
By dawn it is done. We emerge to the scent of snapped limbs
and mangled trees that line the street in heaps of green.

The new world is unwell. Unripe mast is harvested too soon.
Green acorns cling to the litter of white oak trees.
Small nodules bead the broken stems beneath the leaves
of a southern red. Let them return their tannins to earth.

In the forest, root balls of red clay mark new clearings—
a score of northern red oak down, upended by weight and wind.
Saplings of green ash begin their sprint to light.
The pungent air is ripe with rot.

Blue-green needles of a loblolly stand mingle with conelettes
of shortleaf pine. They spike the nose with an acrid clean.
Green gum balls litter dirt with a latent grace.
Still air is sweet but laced with death.

Here in the gently rolling Georgia hills,
her new growth woods rising over red clay,
her ragged fields recovering from cotton,
the forgotten graves of warriors and slaves—

our world is a shattered, fragrant place. We live
in the wake of voracious storms. Beyond our borders
I see bodies littering beaches, and the tortured eyes
of a lost child wracked by what we unleashed.

The wind has softened. Light slants
through scudding clouds. Death sparkles
in shafts of sun. Some things will never wash clean
so we light a scented candle and sing.

To Bring You Beauty

I would bring you beauty
if I only knew how.
I would slip into spirit,

dissolve into autumn breeze
which carries the scent
of crimson sage

to clouds of yellow butterflies
in the afternoon light
of their lives.

I'd hover with a bumblebee
in the spell of a purple aster
then drift in scented air

on a lilting riff of mockingbird-song,
the swerve of a skipper,
a toddler's giggle

through the elusive realm
where beauty infuses all being.
I would bring you a portion

but, reaching, it slips
through re-embodied hands
and recedes like time itself,

its lingering afterglow
reflected in clouds
of evening gnats.

Driving Home After My Fifty-Year Reunion

A soft rain bathes the dry pines of Carolina
  as I drive down a lonely road
    into another autumn.

Farewell old loves.
You spoke your truths, and I
shared mine. The world bleeds for something new.

Cloudless sulphurs flutter over brown fields,
  across winding backroads,
    onto goldenrod shoulders.

Goodbye, mates, perhaps
forever. It is fall. For some
their last.

Still, the sun sparkles from roadside puddles
  and woodland sunflowers shine
    like a fresh van Gogh.

We parted in the glow of youth—
while warriors rode the fiery horse to far-off wars
we dreamers marched chaotic streets to conjure peace.

Today, a living mist soothes the trees.
  Stubble covers sandy fields.
    Soy fades to pale.

Old friends, did we tame
our feral souls at last? We have
striven. Soon, with grace, we yield.

A Close Encounter with an Old Field

It’s just an old field.
I have been back more than once,
perplexed

at how ordinary
in the light of late afternoon,
or morning, or the glare of noon.

It’s gone.
Whatever was is not now.
It seems a shame, the un-tame rush

replaced by shrug
and stolen glance
at time,

the slow ride home for reheated leftovers
to sustain my aging.
It was fall

when I went wandering
blazed paths through the pungent hush
of hickory, beech, and white oak stands

to forest edge at right-of-way
cut straight across the curve of hills
where I stood blinking back the light—

by the sun-splashed shores
of an old field grown wild
breaking over asphalt slabs

which once went somewhere
beyond the post hole fence
that vainly holds back green

swells of sumac and thistle
tangled in turbulence
sparkling in the silent roar

Of a thin place opening
onto an emerald sea

in the presence of which
I would remove my shoes
wash my soul in sunlight

and float the timeless warmth
to a new heaven
and a new Earth.

But that was all, and over soon,
just slant of light and insect drone,
no still small voice that could be heard

above the buzz and background trill.
So was it somehow up to me
to say aloud what hangs in air?

All flesh is grass, its beauty as
the flower of the field

that dies with fall—been said by better
than one who wanted just right then
no more than *now* and this sweet Earth

of distant laughter, lovers strolling,
mothers holding tiny hands
by grandpas lost in memories

reliving childhood running free.
Right there beneath the freshening breeze
a shadow passed inside of me:

You know your heart
not that of mine

And in the sudden hush I heard
a hymn of weeds
set in my mind:

Take the sun and set your roots,
soften earth and heal the scars

For several seasons I've returned, but
never caught the song again, never learned
what sang from the silence inside.

Heron in the Woods

We loved that bird—how once
he'd launch his four-foot frame
to glide above the mud and pools,

the weathered rocks and rotting logs.
How once he'd stand amid the muck
plucking silver shards of life.

So what compelled his final flight
from riverbanks sustaining life
to the hush of lowland woods?

Some may claim birds have no soul
(they say the same of you and me),
but say not knowing one bird well.

Do you not sense a presence
more than hollow bones
and handsome feathers?

Can you not see through the dimming eyes
of a wild bird waiting in the woods
for what must come in morning

shadows where love and resignation
forge bonds beyond kind?
Silver feathers grace the ground

that launched his soul to final flight
to soar above what lies behind
on woodland floor and in my mind.

Let the Season of Leaf-Fall Begin

A cool wind blew in overnight
and now my oaks are raining acorns.

Dry leaves crunch underfoot
as I shuffle out to the street.

And so the season of leaf-fall begins
with the *scritch* of rake on the driveway

and a glance at the canopy overhead.
The greens of countless leaves remain,

though some have gone senescent.
While tulip trees are teasing yellow

and dogwoods trend rose-orange,
peak season is weeks away.

As trees drain green from dormant leaves
they reveal their underlying hues.

Their dazzle was always a layer beneath
subsumed by the business of summer.

Just so as human years accrete—
when we've served our purpose and hurried on

to the grace unveiled in our waning,
may we savor our season of letting go.

Today I leave my task half done
to sit out back and stare at trees.

I'm not the man I used to be,
but more of what I always was.

The Ache at the Edge of Autumn

Heaven drifts in on an autumn day
  when dry leaves filter long moments
    and the very air caresses the land,

when boundaries collapse and being extends
  until all is kindness, dappled
    in afternoon light.

You inhabit a living songscape
  and hear the choir of the wood cricket
    humming an ode to existence itself.

A fresh wind renews the sky.
  The river course restores its water.
    A romp of otters slips upstream.

The whole of life has brought you here—
  time, fulfilled in a moment of joy.
    Consummation always comes

and afternoon forever fades.
  There's an ache at the edge of an autumn day
    when time trends toward waning

and Earth spins ever away.
  There's an ache an octave above pain
    a register beyond joy

built in the core of creation
forged in the fire of the long-ago making
when the great winding down began.

There’s an ache impressed on the cosmic tapestry
through the ever-expanding void.
I am is its cry, ever fading.

There’s an urge to return that is etched on us all
but home is a haven gracing the past.
Do you feel the ache inside your soul?

It burns but does not consume.
Heaven is somewhere adjacent to here.
Eternity dances the edges of fall.

The Harmonics of Fall

When social loops resonate
to unholy harmonics in a world
wired close and wound tight.

When the soundtrack of triumph
sweeps your people, and sweet
ideals are wielded as weapons.

When the grievance is just
too great to ignore and your mind
is gripped in anger—go.

Go into an autumn afternoon
where out of stillness, peace
descends on dry leaf flurries.

Where a thousand blackbirds
speak in tongues of tiny angels
timeless blessings to life.

Where echoes of ageless minds
penetrate prepackaged lives
and strife recedes to hush.

When impelled by honor to act—
engage, but withhold your soul,
for you are more than your role.

You have felt the autumn breeze.
You've sensed the inner harmony.
You have been blessed by birds.

For One More Flower

She was foraging a mid-autumn meadow
for one more flower in the fading light
when a cooling breeze began to blow
as late day slipped into chill of night.

Beneath a billion dying stars
in a deep black sky, a tiny soul
dims in a bumblebee body
latched to a tenuous bloom.

Perhaps she'll see another dawn
where a kind sun warms the dew-wet weeds
as she wakes to a golden-yellow dream
washed in the fragrance of fall

where the final flower of a now-dead day
will serve the first nectar of morning.

The Grace of Late Autumn

Mine the mellow Southern season
   mixing mild with bracing days,
when woodlands open up to welcome
   winter's heart of tan and brown.

There's peace in piercing shafts of sunlight
   slowly warming a forest floor
where solemn anoles fade in silence,
   green to tan in golden sun.

There's grace in shy suburban does
   when flushed from front yard
flower gardens—gracile statues
   snapped to life

                        and soaring lightly

through the early
      evening shadows
         cast by a rising
            Hunter's Moon.

November brings a soul of sweetness
   wrapped in dwindling light and life,
a respite from the web of strife
   and grace to buffer what's to come.

Last November Sunset

Glade Farmhouse, Georgia

November's moon which lit long nights
is just a ghostly crescent slowly
sinking in the western sky.

I watch the sunset flare, then fade
as crimson clouds darken to shadows
hugging the stubble horizon.

Off a distant ridge, December
wind clears warmth
from a once promising day

and the heart of a hundred billion stars
smears cold light
across velvet silence.

A spare beauty bears the hint
of primal heat
through widening gulfs

to fallow souls rooted in lost time
waiting for winter
to spring new seed from sweet decline.

End Times, Again

As light drains from another year
I hear the hymn of insects dwindle.
Days diminish. Cycles reset. End times

have come again. Passion-vines
bear yellowed fruit and withered leaves,
which late-season caterpillars scour

in vain. Soon, the chrysalis confronts
the cold. Bumblebee colonies collapse.
Weary queens abandon their hives.

Orphaned workers forage brown fields
in search of nectar. Perhaps an aster
persists somewhere. But home has gone

to seed. Beside the dry depression
where spring pools nursed peepers,
lurid sedges flaunt battle spikes.

Wild rye wields tan spears. Dark pods
hang from senna. The tips of thistles
launch parachutes into November wind.

Ironweed bristles, grasses bend. Blue stems
wave seed tufts like tattered prayer flags.
Today, the hope of new life lies

buried in root and seed bank, tucked
in mud and sleeping queens. But to us
now, the season of culling is come.

To Make a Frost Flower

You could go a whole life
scarcely aware of ephemera.
How frost flowers grace

the morning hours in unkempt
ditches, ragged shoulders,
borders and abandoned fields

that first hard freeze of fall.
Consider the white crownbeard
how it grows. It flourishes

in heat of summer, flowers
ugly early autumn, leaves
a stick carcass standing

barren to the bitter wind
that rattles down the winter.
But come the quiet dawn

when cold envelops open
fields and seeps inside
the hardened earth—

when morning crackles
Frostweed blooms. Up
from old roots, sap bleeds

through breached stems,
   oozing into open air
      as frozen locks of cotton

candy, silver swirls
   of crystal clouds leaven
      the now broken body.

Translucent grace is born
   to morning, gone by noon.
      Wounded by winter, the weed

turns guts to ghostly flowers
   and waits for the inconceivable
      spring to rise again from roots.

EPILOGUE

And when my seasons end at last
as seasons will, I only ask a year's reprieve
to taste of life again, again.

Benediction: May You Grow

May you grow in the soul of each new season
as week by week new flowers unfold—
bloodroot to bluet, jessamine, clover,
gardenia to goldenrod, thistle, and aster.

May you ground your life in the cycles of Earth
as bare dirt yields to new green shoots,
buds to blossoms and tender leaves,
fruit and seeds to stubble and husk.

May you savor the spirit of each new hour
as minute by minute the moments flow—
from pastel dawns to high cotton skies,
slate-roofed noons to obsidian nights.

In seasons, in cycles, each breath and beat,
may you mirror the stillness that rests beneath.

Postlude: A Psalm of Gaia

She leads me beside a vernal pool
where swamp frogs trill the early spring.
Her breath refreshes musty air
and lifts the chill from mud-slick skin.

She turns me loose in a garden world
and weaves a mid-summer feast.
Her leaf-green shadows soothe the days
and a chorus of katydids comforts the nights.

She lays me down in an autumn meadow
bobbing with skippers and bees.
Her gentle sunlight dries the dew
and I feel the warmth on petals and wings.

She takes my hand on winter nights
and guides me down a darkened path.
A thousand stars pierce the sky
and I sense the harsh beauty beyond.

Though the night wind stings my lungs
and ice invades my bones,
through pain I know that life abides,
to kindness life ascends.

About the Author

Bob Ambrose, Jr. is an environmental engineer retired from the U.S. Environmental Protection Agency, Office of Research and Development. He has been writing poetry since 2009 and has been active in the Athens, Georgia Word of Mouth spoken word community. Bob has been the featured reader at events in Athens, Cincinnati, and Austin, including churches, bookshops, bars, and gardens. He presented two multimedia poetry readings at the 2025 Wild Goose Festival in Harmony, NC.

Bob's first book, *Journey to Embarkation—A Reflection in Poetry* (Parson's Porch Books, 2016), looks back on his life as a journey, reflecting on departures and encounters along the way. His second book, *Between Birdsong and Boulder—Poems on the Life of Gaia* (Kelsay Books, 2024), covers the science-based story of the cosmos in lyric form. Bob lives with his wife by the Oconee River in Athens, and travels to England to visit his daughter's family and indulge his two granddaughters.

Websites:
birdsongboulder.com
thirteen-moons.com

www.ingramcontent.com/pod-product-compliance
Lightning Source LLC
LaVergne TN
LVHW010623100826
845148LV00014B/3077